A
# Betty Crocker
## PICTURE COOKBOOK
# CASSEROLES
### Range-Top and Oven

## GOLDEN PRESS/NEW YORK
Western Publishing Company, Inc.
Racine, Wisconsin

Copyright © 1982, 1975 by General Mills, Inc., Minneapolis, Minn.
All rights reserved. Produced in the U.S.A.

Library of Congress Catalog Card Number: 81-83379
ISBN 0-307-09666-1

Golden® and Golden Press® are trademarks of
Western Publishing Company, Inc.

# CONTENTS

**EGGPLANT**, available year round, is most abundant in August and September. Look for a pear-shaped plant, 3 to 6 inches across, dark and glossy color with no blemishes. Eggplant contains minerals and vitamins as well as protein. It is delicious with meats, tomatoes, cheese, sour cream, yogurt and mushrooms.

# Beef-Eggplant Bake

- 1- pound beef round steak, ½ inch thick, cut into 1½ x ¼-inch strips
- 1 tablespoon vegetable oil
- 1 can (8 ounces) tomato sauce
- 1 can (6 ounces) tomato paste
- ½ cup water
- 1 medium onion, chopped (about ½ cup)
- 1 medium green pepper, chopped (about 1 cup)
- 1 teaspoon salt
- 1 teaspoon garlic salt
- 1 teaspoon dried oregano leaves
- ½ teaspoon dried basil leaves
- 1 package (9 ounces) frozen Italian green beans
- 1 medium eggplant, pared and cut into ¼-inch slices
- 1 cup shredded mozzarella cheese (about 4 ounces)
- ¼ cup grated Parmesan cheese

Brown beef round steak strips in oil in 10-inch skillet over medium heat. Stir in tomato sauce, tomato paste, water, onion, green pepper, salt, garlic salt, oregano and basil. Heat to boiling; reduce heat. Cover and simmer 30 minutes.

Heat oven to 350°. Rinse frozen beans under running cold water to separate. Layer half each of the eggplant slices, beans and beef mixture in ungreased 2-quart casserole; repeat. Cover and bake 50 minutes.

Sprinkle casserole with cheeses. Bake uncovered until cheese is melted and golden, about 5 minutes. Let stand 5 minutes before serving.    6 SERVINGS.

Coat beef with flour; pound beef with mallet to tenderize.

Brown beef in skillet; push beef to side and add onion.

Pour the potato liquid mixture on beef and onion in skillet.

Rinse beans quickly under running cold water to separate.

# Saucy Steak Skillet

1- pound beef boneless round steak, cut into
    serving pieces
¼ cup all-purpose flour
1 tablespoon vegetable oil
1 large onion, chopped (about 1 cup)
1 can (16 ounces) whole potatoes, drained
    (reserve liquid)
¼ cup catsup
1 tablespoon Worcestershire sauce
2 teaspoons bell pepper flakes
1 teaspoon instant beef bouillon
1 teaspoon salt
½ teaspoon dried marjoram leaves
¼ teaspoon pepper
1 package (10 ounces) frozen Italian green
    beans
1 jar (2 ounces) sliced pimiento, drained

Coat beef steak pieces with flour; pound into beef. Brown
beef in oil in 10-inch skillet; push beef to side. Cook and
stir onion in oil until tender; drain.

Add enough water to reserved potato liquid to measure 1
cup. Mix potato liquid, catsup, Worcestershire sauce, pepper flakes, instant bouillon, salt, marjoram and pepper;
pour on beef and onion. Heat to boiling; reduce heat. Cover
and simmer until beef is tender, 1¼ to 1½ hours.

Rinse frozen beans under running cold water to separate.
Add potatoes, beans and pimiento to skillet. Heat to boiling; reduce heat. Cover and simmer until beans are tender,
10 to 15 minutes.    4 SERVINGS.

# Hearty Chili

1 medium green pepper, chopped (about 1 cup)
2 medium onions, chopped (about 1 cup)
1 clove garlic, crushed
1 tablespoon vegetable oil
1 pound beef stew meat, cut into ½-inch pieces
3 tablespoons flour
2 tablespoons vegetable oil
2 cans (28 ounces each) whole tomatoes, drained and cut into fourths (see note)
3 cans (16 ounces each) kidney beans
1 can (8 ounces) tomato sauce
1 to 2 tablespoons chili powder
2 teaspoons salt

Cook and stir green pepper, onions and garlic in 1 tablespoon oil in Dutch oven over medium heat until onions are tender, about 5 minutes; remove from Dutch oven. Coat beef stew meat with flour; brown in 2 tablespoons oil.

Stir in tomatoes, beans (with liquid), tomato sauce, chili powder, green pepper mixture and salt. Heat to boiling; reduce heat. Cover and simmer, stirring occasionally, until beef is tender, about 2 hours. Uncover and simmer, stirring occasionally, 30 minutes.   10 SERVINGS.

*Note:* If you like a thinner consistency, do not drain tomatoes.

Cut the tomatoes into fourths with scissors.

Peel garlic clove; crush with garlic press.

Or chop peeled garlic clove on cutting board.

Brown flour-coated meat in vegetable oil.

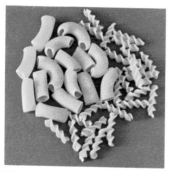

Rigatoni, spiral macaroni.

Mostaccioli, shell macaroni.

# Roman Country Beef Dinner

1½ pounds beef stew meat, cut into 1-inch
    pieces
2 tablespoons vegetable oil
1 can (29 ounces) whole tomatoes
1 can (8 ounces) tomato sauce
3 cups water
1 large onion, chopped (about 1 cup)
2 teaspoons salt
½ teaspoon dried oregano leaves
½ teaspoon dried thyme leaves
4 ounces uncooked large macaroni
    (rigatoni, mostaccioli, shell or spiral)
1 package (10 ounces) frozen cut green
    beans
Grated Parmesan cheese

Brown beef stew meat in oil in Dutch oven; drain. Stir in tomatoes (with liquid), tomato sauce, water, onion, salt, oregano and thyme. Heat to boiling; reduce heat. Cover and simmer until beef is almost tender, 1½ to 2 hours.

Stir in macaroni. Heat to boiling; reduce heat. Cover and simmer, stirring occasionally, until macaroni is almost tender, about 20 minutes.

Rinse frozen beans under running cold water to separate. Stir beans into beef mixture; cook uncovered until beans are tender, 15 to 20 minutes. Sprinkle with cheese.

6 SERVINGS.

# Hearty Roast and Vegetables

2½- to 3-pound beef chuck pot roast
1 teaspoon seasoned salt
½ teaspoon dried marjoram leaves
¼ teaspoon celery seed
¼ teaspoon pepper
1 clove garlic, finely chopped
½ cup water
1 package (10 ounces) frozen Brussels
   sprouts
4 medium carrots, cut into 3x½-inch strips
2 medium potatoes, cut into 1-inch slices
2 medium turnips, cut into eighths
1 medium onion, sliced
½ teaspoon salt

Trim excess fat from beef pot roast. Rub Dutch oven with fat cut from beef; brown beef in Dutch oven. Sprinkle with seasoned salt, marjoram, celery seed, pepper and garlic; add water. Heat to boiling; reduce heat. Cover and simmer 1½ hours.

Rinse frozen Brussels sprouts under running cold water to separate. Add vegetables to Dutch oven, placing Brussels sprouts on top; sprinkle with salt. If necessary, add ¼ cup water. Heat to boiling; reduce heat. Cover and simmer until beef and vegetables are tender, 30 to 40 minutes. Sprinkle with parsley.    4 TO 6 SERVINGS.

# Mañana Beef Bake

1 pound ground beef
1 large onion, chopped (about 1 cup)
1 can (10¾ ounces) condensed cream of
   chicken soup
1 can (4 ounces) mushroom stems and
   pieces
¾ cup milk
1 small green pepper, chopped (about ½
   cup)
½ cup sliced pitted ripe olives
2 tablespoons soy sauce
2 teaspoons Worcestershire sauce
⅛ teaspoon pepper
5 ounces noodles, cooked and drained
1 cup shredded sharp Cheddar cheese (about
   4 ounces)

Cook and stir ground beef and onion in 10-inch skillet until beef is light brown; drain. Stir in soup, mushrooms (with liquid), milk, green pepper, olives, soy sauce, Worcestershire sauce and pepper.

Line 2-quart casserole with piece of heavy-duty aluminum foil. Pour noodles and beef mixture into foil-lined casserole; sprinkle with cheese. Seal foil securely; freeze until solid, 20 to 24 hours.

Remove foil-wrapped frozen block from casserole and label; freeze up to 3 weeks.

■24 hours before serving, unwrap frozen beef mixture and place in 2-quart casserole; cover and thaw in refrigerator.

■1 hour 20 minutes before serving, heat oven to 350°. Bake casserole covered 1 hour. Stir; top with 1 cup chow mein noodles and ½ cup mixed salted nuts. Bake uncovered 10 minutes.   8 SERVINGS.

1 small onion equals ¼ cup chopped onion or 1 tablespoon (or more) instant minced.

For recipes low in liquid, soak instant minced onion in equal amount of water 3 minutes.

# Spaghetti Chop Chop

½ pound ground beef*
½ pound pork bulk sausage*
1 medium green pepper
2 cups hot cooked spaghetti (about 4 ounces uncooked)
1 can (16 ounces) Chinese vegetables, drained
1 can (10¾ ounces) condensed cream of shrimp soup
1 can (8 ounces) water chestnuts, drained and sliced
1 can (4½ ounces) mushroom stems and pieces, drained
½ cup water
1 small onion, finely chopped (about ¼ cup)
1 teaspoon salt
¾ cup shredded sharp cheese (about 3 ounces)

Heat oven to 375°. Cook and stir ground beef and pork bulk sausage until light brown, 15 to 20 minutes; drain. Slice 3 rings from green pepper; reserve rings for garnish. Chop remaining green pepper.

Stir chopped green pepper and remaining ingredients except cheese into meat. Pour into ungreased 2-quart casserole; sprinkle with cheese. Bake uncovered 30 minutes. Top with green pepper rings; bake 5 minutes.   6 SERVINGS.

*1 pound ground beef can be substituted for the mixture of ground beef and pork sausage.

You can remove the fat from ground beef with baster.

Or skim fat from ground beef with large spoon.

Or remove ground beef with slotted spoon and pour off fat.

Or use slotted cover to hold beef while you pour off fat.

# Deep Dish Hamburger Pie

1 pound ground beef
2 teaspoons instant minced onion
2 teaspoons chili powder
1 teaspoon dried oregano leaves
1 can (10¾ ounces) condensed tomato soup
1 can (16 ounces) sliced carrots, drained
1 can (12 ounces) vacuum-pack whole kernel
   corn
Sesame Topping (below)

Heat oven to 400°. Cook and stir ground beef over medium heat until light brown; drain. Place beef in ungreased baking dish, 11¾x7½x1¾ inches. Stir in onion, chili powder, oregano, soup, carrots and corn.

Drop Sesame Topping by teaspoonfuls around edges of baking dish. Bake uncovered until topping is golden brown, about 15 minutes.   6 SERVINGS.

## SESAME TOPPING

1 cup biscuit baking mix
¼ cup butter or margarine, softened
3 tablespoons boiling water
2 tablespoons sesame seed

Mix all ingredients until a soft dough forms.

---

### S-T-R-E-E-T-C-H IT TWO WAYS!

You can make Sesame Topping double as a pie crust. Pat the dough with floured hands into a 9-inch pie plate, bringing the pastry to the edge of the pan. Flute the edge if you like; do not prick. Bake in a 450° oven 10 minutes. Cool, and it's ready for your favorite filling.

---

# Beef Balls Provençale

1 pound ground beef
1 egg
1 small onion, chopped (about ¼ cup)
⅓ cup dry bread crumbs
¼ cup milk
1 teaspoon salt
1 teaspoon Worcestershire sauce
⅛ teaspoon pepper
1 tablespoon vegetable oil
Vegetables Provençale (below)
Grated Parmesan or Romano cheese

Mix all ingredients except oil, Vegetables Provençale and cheese. Shape mixture by tablespoonfuls into 1½-inch balls. (For ease in shaping meatballs, wet hands with cold water occasionally.) Cook meatballs in oil in 12-inch skillet over medium heat until light brown on all sides; remove from skillet. Drain fat from skillet.

Prepare Vegetables Provençale. Top with meatballs. Heat to boiling; reduce heat. Cover and simmer until vegetables are crisp-tender, 10 to 15 minutes. Sprinkle with cheese. 4 SERVINGS.

## VEGETABLES PROVENCALE

4 small zucchini, cut into ½-inch slices
1 small eggplant, pared and cut into ½-inch pieces (about 2½ cups)
1 medium onion, sliced
2 cloves garlic, finely chopped
1 can (16 ounces) stewed tomatoes
1 teaspoon salt
½ teaspoon dried oregano leaves

Mix all ingredients in 12-inch skillet.

# Hot Tamale Bake

1 cup yellow cornmeal
1 cup cold water
2 cups boiling water
1 tablespoon butter or margarine
1 teaspoon salt
1 pound ground beef
2 small onions, sliced
½ medium green pepper, chopped (about
    ½ cup)
3 tablespoons yellow cornmeal
1 can (16 ounces) whole tomatoes
1 can (16 ounces) kidney beans, drained
1 to 2 teaspoons chili powder
1 teaspoon salt
½ teaspoon crushed dried chilies
¼ teaspoon garlic salt
½ cup shredded taco-flavored or Cheddar
    cheese (about 2 ounces)
Shredded lettuce

Heat oven to 350°. Mix 1 cup cornmeal and the cold water in 2-quart saucepan. Stir in boiling water, butter and 1 teaspoon salt. Cook over medium heat, stirring constantly, until mixture thickens and bubbles; reduce heat. Cover and simmer 5 minutes, stirring occasionally. Spread evenly over bottom and side of greased 3-quart casserole. Bake uncovered 15 minutes.

While cornmeal crust is baking, prepare filling. Cook and stir ground beef over medium heat until light brown; drain. Stir in onions, green pepper, 3 tablespoons cornmeal, the tomatoes (with liquid), beans, chili powder, 1 teaspoon salt, the chilies and garlic salt. Pour into crust; sprinkle with cheese. Bake uncovered until bubbly, about 35 minutes. Serve on lettuce in bowls.     8 SERVINGS.

First cut rutabaga into ½-inch slices, then sticks.

Drop dough by spoonfuls onto ribs (not into liquid).

# Short Ribs and Herb Dumplings

   3 **pounds beef short ribs**
   2 **cups water**
   1 **teaspoon salt**
   1 **teaspoon instant beef bouillon**
  ⅛ **teaspoon pepper**
   1 **bay leaf**
   1 **medium rutabaga, cut into ½-inch sticks**
   2 **medium onions, cut into fourths**
  ½ **teaspoon salt**
    **Herb Dumplings (right)**
   1 **package (10 ounces) frozen green peas**

Trim excess fat from beef short ribs. Brown beef in 12-inch skillet or Dutch oven; drain. Add water, 1 teaspoon salt, the instant bouillon, pepper and bay leaf. Heat to boiling; reduce heat. Cover and simmer, stirring occasionally, 1 hour.

Skim fat from broth. Add rutabaga and onions; sprinkle with ½ teaspoon salt. Heat to boiling; reduce heat. Cover and simmer until rutabaga is almost tender, 30 to 40 minutes.

Prepare Herb Dumplings. Drop dumpling dough by spoonfuls onto beef as pictured. Cook uncovered over medium heat 10 minutes.

Rinse frozen peas under running cold water to separate. Sprinkle peas around dumplings. Cover and cook 10 minutes. Remove ribs, dumplings and peas with slotted spoon and arrange on serving platter. Serve with pan juices, skimming off fat if necessary.    4 SERVINGS.

## HERB DUMPLINGS

Mix 1 cup biscuit baking mix, ⅓ cup milk and ¼ teaspoon poultry seasoning until a soft dough forms.

Spoon half of the potato mixture into the casserole.

Cover with the cut-up cooked corned beef and cheese.

# Potato Reuben Casserole

Instant mashed potato puffs (enough for 8
   servings)
1 can (16 ounces) sauerkraut, drained
2 green onions, thinly sliced (about ¼ cup)
2 cups cut-up cooked corned beef
4 ounces Swiss cheese, cut up (about 1 cup)
   Paprika

Heat oven to 350°. Prepare potato puffs in 3-quart saucepan
as directed on package. Stir in sauerkraut and onions.
Spoon half of the potato-sauerkraut mixture into ungreased 2-quart casserole; cover with corned beef and
cheese. Top with remaining potato-sauerkraut mixture;
sprinkle with paprika. Bake uncovered 30 minutes.
6 SERVINGS.

**Irish Corned Beef Casserole:** Substitute 4 cups shredded
cabbage for the sauerkraut. Cook cabbage in ½ cup boiling
water and ½ teaspoon salt just until tender, 8 to 10
minutes; drain. Add to potato puffs as directed.

---

### A NOTE ON REFRIGERATION

When you cook a large cut of meat or a big chicken
or turkey, and you plan to refrigerate it for later
use, be sure to:

1. Cool quickly, cover and refrigerate.
2. Cool, cover and refrigerate cooking liquids.
3. Refrigerate poultry, dressing and gravy sepa-
   rately.
4. Use meat within 3 days, poultry within 2 days.
5. Freeze for longer storage.

# Pork Chop Scallop

6 to 8 pork chops, ½ to ¾ inch thick
1 teaspoon salt
2 cups water
2 medium carrots, thinly sliced (about 1 cup)
1 package (10 ounces) frozen Italian green
   beans
2 tablespoons butter or margarine
1 package (5.5 ounces) scalloped potatoes
1 can (10¾ ounces) condensed cream of
   celery soup
⅔ cup milk
½ teaspoon dried basil leaves
½ teaspoon Worcestershire sauce

Heat oven to 350°. Trim excess fat from pork chops. Rub skillet with fat trimmed from pork. Brown pork in skillet; sprinkle with salt. Heat water to boiling in 3-quart saucepan. Add carrots and frozen beans; heat to boiling. Stir in butter and potato slices and Sauce Mix from scalloped potatoes package.

Mix soup, milk, basil and Worcestershire sauce; stir into vegetable mixture. Pour into ungreased baking dish, 13½x8¾x1¾ inches. Place pork on top. Cover and bake 45 minutes.

Uncover and bake until pork is tender, 10 to 15 minutes. Let stand 5 minutes before serving.    6 TO 8 SERVINGS.

**Timing Tip:** If you want to serve at different times, after baking, reduce oven temperature to 150° and cover with aluminum foil. Pork Chop Scallop will hold up to 45 minutes.

Stir soup mixture into vegetable mixture in saucepan.

Place pork chops on top in baking dish; cover and bake.

# Pork Paprika

---

 1 can (16 ounces) sauerkraut, drained
 3 medium potatoes, shredded
 ½ cup milk
 ½ teaspoon salt
 ⅛ teaspoon pepper
 1 pound bacon, crisply fried and crumbled
 1 medium onion, thinly sliced
 1 pound smoked pork shoulder roll, thinly
   sliced (see note)
1½ cups dry white wine
 1 tablespoon paprika
 2 tablespoons snipped parsley

Heat oven to 400°. Mix sauerkraut, potatoes, milk, salt and
pepper. Spread half of the mixture in ungreased baking
dish, 13½x8¾x1¾ inches. Reserve ⅓ cup of the bacon.
Layer remaining bacon, the onion and pork slices on sauerkraut mixture in baking dish. Top with remaining sauerkraut mixture.

Pour wine on sauerkraut mixture; sprinkle with reserved bacon and the paprika. Cover and bake 1 hour. Let stand 10 minutes before serving. Sprinkle with parsley.
8 SERVINGS.

*Note:* Packaged smoked pork shoulder roll usually comes in 2-pound size or larger. Remaining pork can be thinly sliced and broiled or panfried, or simmered whole in water until light brown (40 minutes per pound).

This dish was created using the sour and salty combinations that are typical of Philippine cooking.

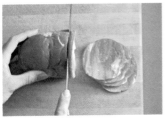
One pound pork shoulder roll serves eight in this recipe.

Spread half of the sauerkraut mixture in the baking dish.

Add all but ⅓ cup bacon, then the onion and pork slices.

Add the remaining sauerkraut, wine, bacon and paprika.

# Pork Steak Dinner in a Dish

4 pork blade or arm steaks, about ½ inch thick
10 small new potatoes (about 1 pound)
1 small onion, chopped (about ¼ cup)
1 can (10¾ ounces) condensed cream of
   chicken soup
1 can (2 ounces) mushroom stems and pieces
2 tablespoons dry sherry (optional)
½ teaspoon garlic salt
½ teaspoon Worcestershire sauce
¼ teaspoon dried thyme leaves
1 package (10 ounces) frozen green peas and
   carrots

Brown pork steaks in 10-inch skillet; drain. Add potatoes and onion. Mix soup, mushrooms (with liquid), sherry, garlic salt, Worcestershire sauce and thyme. Pour on pork, potatoes and onion. Heat to boiling; reduce heat. Cover and simmer until tender, 50 to 60 minutes.

Rinse frozen peas and carrots under running cold water to separate; add to pork and vegetables. Cover and simmer until peas and carrots are tender, 10 to 15 minutes.
4 SERVINGS.

Brown the pork steaks, two at a time, in skillet.

Pour soup mixture on pork, potatoes and onion.

**OKRA** is an edible pod that is used in soups and stews. It combines well with other vegetables, and is especially good with tomatoes. Okra is available fresh, canned and frozen. The peak months for fresh okra are June through October. When buying fresh okra, choose bright green pods 2 to 4 inches in length.

# Saskatchewan Succotash

1½ pounds Canadian-style bacon, cut into
    ½-inch slices
  1 can (16 ounces) whole tomatoes
  1 teaspoon salt
  ½ teaspoon dried marjoram leaves
  ¼ teaspoon pepper
  1 package (10 ounces) frozen baby lima
    beans
1½ cups ½-inch slices fresh okra or 1 package
    (10 ounces) frozen okra
  1 can (12 ounces) vacuum-pack whole
    kernel corn

Brown Canadian-style bacon slices in 12-inch skillet or Dutch oven; drain. Mix tomatoes (with liquid), salt, marjoram and pepper; pour on bacon. Heat to boiling; reduce heat. Cover and simmer 15 minutes.

Remove bacon from skillet. Rinse frozen lima beans under running cold water to separate. Add lima beans, okra and corn to skillet; top with bacon. Heat to boiling; reduce heat. Cover and simmer until vegetables are tender, 10 to 15 minutes.   6 SERVINGS.

# Pork with Crunchy Dumplings

- 1 package (10 ounces) frozen baby lima beans
- 1 can (12 ounces) pork luncheon loaf, cut into ¾-inch pieces
- 1 jar (2 ounces) pimiento, chopped (about 3 tablespoons)
- 1 can (11 ounces) condensed Cheddar cheese soup
- 1 cup water
- 1 teaspoon instant minced onion
- ¼ teaspoon dry mustard
- ½ teaspoon Worcestershire sauce
  Crunchy Dumplings (below)

Heat oven to 425°. Rinse frozen beans under running cold water to separate. Layer beans, pork pieces and pimiento in ungreased 2-quart casserole. Mix soup, water, onion, dry mustard and Worcestershire sauce; pour over pork, beans and pimiento. Bake uncovered 30 minutes.

While casserole is baking, prepare Crunchy Dumplings. Remove casserole from oven and spoon 7 or 8 dumplings onto hot mixture. Bake uncovered until dumplings are golden brown, 20 to 25 minutes.   6 SERVINGS.

## CRUNCHY DUMPLINGS
- 1 cup all-purpose flour
- 2 teaspoons baking powder
- 1 tablespoon instant minced onion
- ½ cup coarsely chopped cocktail peanuts
- ¼ teaspoon salt
- ½ cup milk
- 2 tablespoons vegetable oil

Mix flour, baking powder, onion, peanuts and salt; add milk and oil. Stir until a soft dough forms.

Cut pork luncheon loaf into bite-size pieces.

Add peanuts to dumplings for crunch and protein.

Stir dumpling mixture until a soft dough forms.

Dip spoon in gravy; dumpling won't stick to spoon.

Add the Swiss cheese to the onion sauce and ham.

Alternate noodles and sauce mixture in casserole.

# Ham and Green Noodle Bake

1 medium onion, chopped (about ½ cup)
2 tablespoons butter or margarine
2 tablespoons flour
½ teaspoon salt
¼ teaspoon pepper
¼ teaspoon dry mustard
1¾ cups milk*
2 cups cut-up fully cooked ham
½ cup shredded Swiss cheese (about 2 ounces)
4 ounces uncooked spinach egg noodles
2 tablespoons grated Parmesan cheese
Twist of lemon
Celery leaves

Heat oven to 375°. Cook and stir onion in butter until tender. Blend in flour, salt, pepper and mustard. Heat over low heat, stirring constantly, until bubbly; remove from heat. Add milk; heat to boiling, stirring constantly. Boil and stir 1 minute. Stir in ham and Swiss cheese.

Cook noodles as directed on package; drain. Alternate layers of noodles and sauce mixture in ungreased 1½-quart casserole; sprinkle with Parmesan cheese. Bake uncovered until bubbly and light brown, about 20 minutes. Garnish with twist of lemon and celery leaves.

6 SERVINGS.

* ¼ cup dry sherry can be substituted for ¼ cup of the milk.

Line bottom and side of greased casserole with cheese slices to within 1 inch of top.

Sprinkle the casserole with chopped walnuts. Shred remaining cheese for garnish.

# Cheese-Ham Bake

About 1 pound Gouda cheese
1 pound fully cooked ham, cut into 1-inch pieces
3 cups cooked rice
1 can (10¾ ounces) condensed cream of chicken soup
2 medium tomatoes, peeled and chopped
1 medium onion, chopped (about ½ cup)
1 medium green pepper, coarsely chopped
1 teaspoon salt
1 cup coarsely chopped walnuts

Heat oven to 350°. Cut cheese into enough ¼-inch-thick slices to line bottom and side of greased 3-quart casserole to within 1 inch of top. Reserve remaining cheese. Mix ham, rice, soup, tomatoes, onion, green pepper and salt; pour into casserole. Sprinkle with walnuts. Shred remaining cheese; sprinkle over walnuts. Bake uncovered until hot and bubbly, 50 minutes to 1 hour. 8 SERVINGS.

# Lamb Andalusian

    4 slices bacon, cut into 1-inch pieces
1½ pounds lean boneless lamb, cut into
        1-inch pieces
    2 medium onions, chopped (about 1 cup)
    2 cloves garlic, finely chopped
    1 can (6 ounces) pitted ripe olives, drained
2½ cups water
    1 cup bulgur
    3 strips orange peel
    1 leek or 2 green onions, chopped
    2 teaspoons instant chicken bouillon
    1 teaspoon dried rosemary leaves
    ½ teaspoon salt
    ½ teaspoon ground cloves
    ¼ teaspoon pepper
    1 package (10 ounces) frozen green peas

Fry bacon pieces in Dutch oven over medium heat until limp. Stir in lamb pieces, onions and garlic. Cook and stir until lamb is brown; drain. Stir in remaining ingredients except peas. Heat to boiling; reduce heat. Cover and simmer until lamb is tender, about 1½ hours.

If necessary, skim fat from broth. Rinse frozen peas under running cold water to separate; stir into casserole. (If thinner consistency is desired, add small amount hot water.) Heat to boiling; reduce heat. Cover and simmer until peas are tender, about 10 minutes.    4 TO 6 SERVINGS.

**LAMB STEW MEAT** is usually cut from the shoulder section (shoulder cut, pictured top left, arm cut or blade cut), the leg section (leg chop, pictured top right) or the neck slices (pictured bottom). If you compare the price per pound of these cuts (including the waste), you may find it cheaper to cut up your own lamb.

# Lamb Casserole

2 small onions, thinly sliced
¼ cup vegetable oil
1 pound lamb stew meat, cut into ½-inch
     pieces
1 small eggplant, pared and sliced
   Salt
   Pepper
1 can (8 ounces) cut green beans, drained
2 medium carrots, sliced
1 large green pepper, cut into rings
4 medium tomatoes, cut into ½-inch slices
2 cups cooked rice
1 cup shredded Cheddar cheese (about 4
     ounces)
   Paprika
2 tablespoons snipped parsley

Cook and stir onions in oil in 10-inch skillet until onions
are tender; remove from skillet. Cook and stir lamb stew
meat in same skillet until brown; drain.

Heat oven to 350°. Arrange eggplant in ungreased baking
dish, 13½x8¾x1¾ inches. Top with lamb; sprinkle with
salt and pepper. Layer onions, beans, carrots, green pepper
and tomatoes on lamb; sprinkle with salt and pepper.
Cover and bake until lamb is tender, about 1 hour.

Arrange rice by ½ cupfuls in 4 diagonal strips on casserole. Top rice with cheese; sprinkle with paprika. Bake
uncovered until cheese is melted, about 15 minutes. Sprinkle with parsley.    6 TO 8 SERVINGS.

# Chicken-Squash Fricassee

2½- to 3-pound broiler-fryer chicken, cut up
2 tablespoons vegetable oil
1½ cups water
2 teaspoons instant chicken bouillon
½ teaspoon dried basil leaves
1 bay leaf
1 pound soft-shelled summer squash
   (crookneck, zucchini or scalloped)
½ pound fresh green beans, cut lengthwise
   into strips or 1 package (9 ounces) frozen
   French-style green beans, thawed
2 medium onions, cut into ½-inch slices
1 teaspoon salt
½ cup pitted ripe olives, drained
1 tablespoon cornstarch
2 tablespoons cold water

Brown chicken pieces in oil in 12-inch skillet or Dutch oven; drain. Add 1½ cups water, the instant bouillon, basil and bay leaf. Heat to boiling; reduce heat. Cover and simmer 30 minutes.

Remove stem and blossom ends from squash, but do not pare. Cut crookneck and zucchini lengthwise in half; cut scalloped crosswise in half. Place squash, beans and onions on chicken. Sprinkle with salt. Heat to boiling; reduce heat. Cover and simmer until chicken is done and vegetables are tender, 20 to 25 minutes.

Remove chicken and vegetables to serving platter; top with olives. Mix cornstarch and 2 tablespoons water; stir into liquid in skillet. Cook over medium heat, stirring constantly, until mixture thickens and boils. Boil and stir 1 minute. Serve over chicken and vegetables.   6 SERVINGS.

Zucchini, yellow crookneck and scalloped squash.

Cut zucchini or crookneck lengthwise in half.

Cut fresh green beans lengthwise into strips.

Place squash, beans and onions on chicken.

Brown chicken pieces on all sides, turning with tongs.

Add the frozen potato slices and asparagus spears.

# Chicken and Vegetable Dinner

⅓ cup all-purpose flour
1 teaspoon salt
1 teaspoon paprika
⅛ teaspoon pepper
2½- to 3-pound broiler-fryer chicken, cut up
3 tablespoons vegetable oil
1½ cups water
½ teaspoon dried savory leaves
¼ teaspoon dried thyme leaves
3 medium carrots, cut into 3x¼-inch strips
½ package (14-ounce size) frozen crinkle-cut
potato slices (about 2 cups)
1 package (10 ounces) frozen asparagus
spears or cuts, broken apart
1½ teaspoons salt

Mix flour, 1 teaspoon salt, the paprika and pepper; coat chicken pieces. Brown chicken in oil in 12-inch skillet or Dutch oven; drain. Add water, savory and thyme. Heat to boiling; reduce heat. Cover and simmer 30 minutes.

Add carrots; cover and simmer 10 minutes. Add frozen potatoes and asparagus; sprinkle with 1½ teaspoons salt. Heat to boiling; reduce heat. Cover and simmer until chicken is done and vegetables are tender, 10 to 15 minutes.     4 TO 6 SERVINGS.

Simmer chicken in water and tomatoes 30 minutes.

Add rice, ham strips, thyme, red pepper and garlic.

# Spanish Chicken and Rice

2½- to 3-pound broiler-fryer chicken, cut up
2 teaspoons salt
¼ teaspoon pepper
2 cans (16 ounces each) stewed tomatoes
1 cup water
1 cup uncooked regular rice
½ pound fully cooked ham, cut into strips
½ teaspoon dried thyme leaves
⅛ to ¼ teaspoon cayenne red pepper
1 clove garlic, crushed
1 package (10 ounces) frozen green peas
1 package (9 ounces) frozen artichoke
    hearts
½ teaspoon salt

Place chicken pieces in 12-inch skillet or Dutch oven; sprinkle with 2 teaspoons salt and the pepper. Pour tomatoes and water on chicken. Heat to boiling; reduce heat. Cover and simmer 30 minutes.

Stir in rice, ham strips, thyme, red pepper and garlic. Heat to boiling; reduce heat. Cover and simmer 20 minutes.

Rinse frozen peas and artichoke hearts under running cold water to separate. Add peas and artichoke hearts to skillet; sprinkle with ½ teaspoon salt. Heat to boiling; reduce heat. Cover and simmer until vegetables are tender, about 10 minutes.    4 SERVINGS.

Layer the vegetables and chicken in 2-quart casserole; prepare cornmeal mixture.

Stir egg yolks, baking powder and seasonings into the luke-warm cornmeal mixture.

Fold the egg whites (beaten just until stiff but not dry) into the cornmeal mixture.

Pour evenly on the green pepper, carefully spreading to edges of the casserole.

# Chicken-Cauliflower Soufflé

- 1 small head cauliflower, broken into ½-inch flowerets
- 1 can (5 ounces) boned chicken, broken into chunks
- 1 medium green pepper, chopped (about ½ cup)
- ¼ teaspoon salt
- 1½ cups milk
- ½ cup cornmeal
- ½ cup shredded Cheddar cheese (about 2 ounces)
- 2 eggs, separated
- 2 teaspoons baking powder
- 1 teaspoon salt
- ¼ teaspoon red pepper sauce
- 1 can (10¾ ounces) condensed tomato soup

Heat oven to 375°. Layer cauliflower, chicken and green pepper in greased 2-quart casserole. Sprinkle with ¼ teaspoon salt.

Heat milk to boiling; stir gradually into cornmeal in medium bowl. Add cheese and stir until mixture is lukewarm. Stir in egg yolks, baking powder, 1 teaspoon salt and the pepper sauce.

Beat egg whites in small mixer bowl just until stiff but not dry; fold into cornmeal mixture. Pour egg white mixture evenly on green pepper; spread to edges of casserole.

Bake uncovered until brown, about 40 minutes. Heat soup over low heat, stirring occasionally, until hot. Serve soup as a sauce with soufflé.     5 SERVINGS.

# Turkey Bake

6 slices bread, cut in half
2 cups cut-up cooked turkey
1 medium onion, chopped (about ½ cup)
1 small green pepper, chopped
2 tablespoons chopped pimiento
½ teaspoon salt
½ teaspoon dried sage leaves, crushed
2 eggs
½ cup mayonnaise or salad dressing
1 cup milk
1 can (10¾ ounces) condensed cream of
    chicken soup

Heat oven to 325°. Layer half of the bread in ungreased baking dish, 8x8x2 inches. Mix turkey, onion, green pepper, pimiento, salt and sage; spread over bread. Top with remaining bread. Beat eggs and mayonnaise; stir in milk and soup. Pour on bread. Sprinkle with paprika. Bake uncovered until casserole is set and top is golden, 1 to 1¼ hours. Serve immediately.    6 SERVINGS.

Spread turkey mixture over bread slices in baking dish.

Pour soup-mayonnaise mixture over top bread layer.

# Tamale Turkey

4 cups cut-up cooked turkey or chicken
1 can (28 ounces) whole tomatoes, drained
(reserve liquid)
1 can (16 ounces) whole kernel corn,
drained (reserve liquid)
1 cup sliced ripe olives
1 medium onion, chopped (about ½ cup)
½ medium green pepper, chopped (about
¼ cup)
2 to 3 tablespoons chili powder
2 tablespoons butter or margarine, softened
1 clove garlic, finely chopped
1 tablespoon salt
1¼ cups yellow cornmeal
4 eggs, beaten
1½ teaspoons instant chicken bouillon
Crushed tortilla chips
Sliced ripe olives

Heat oven to 375°. Mix turkey, tomatoes, corn, olives, onion, green pepper, chili powder, butter, garlic and salt. Add enough water to reserved tomato and corn liquids to measure 1½ cups. Mix liquid, cornmeal, eggs and instant bouillon; stir into turkey mixture. Divide among 10 ungreased individual casseroles.

Bake uncovered until knife inserted in centers comes out clean, about 30 minutes. Garnish with crushed tortilla chips and sliced ripe olives.    10 SERVINGS.

# Deep Dish Turkey Pie

  1 can (23 ounces) vacuum-pack sweet
    potatoes
  2 cups cut-up cooked turkey
  1 medium onion, chopped (about ½ cup)
  1 package (10 ounces) frozen green peas,
    broken apart
  1 package (1 ounce) chicken gravy mix
  1 teaspoon salt
  ½ teaspoon grated lemon peel
    Sweet Potato Biscuits (below)

Heat oven to 400°. Mash enough of the sweet potatoes to measure ¼ cup; reserve for Sweet Potato Biscuits. Cut remaining sweet potatoes into ½-inch slices.

Alternate layers of turkey, onion, frozen peas and sweet potato slices in ungreased 2-quart casserole. Prepare gravy mix as directed on package except—stir in salt and lemon peel; pour into casserole. Bake uncovered 15 minutes.

Prepare Sweet Potato Biscuits dough. Drop half of the dough (5 to 7 spoonfuls) onto hot turkey pie. Bake until biscuit topping is light brown, about 20 minutes.
6 SERVINGS.

### SWEET POTATO BISCUITS
  3 tablespoons shortening
  1 cup all-purpose flour
  ¼ cup mashed sweet potato
  2 teaspoons sugar
  2 teaspoons baking powder
  ½ teaspoon salt
  ¼ to ⅓ cup milk

Cut shortening into flour, sweet potato, sugar, baking powder and salt. Stir in milk. Divide dough in half. Use one half for pie. Drop remaining dough by spoonfuls onto greased baking sheet. Bake until light brown, 12 to 15 minutes.

Cut shortening into the flour mixture with pastry blender.

Add enough milk to the mixture to make a soft dough.

Drop half of dough by spoonfuls onto hot turkey pie.

Drop the remaining dough onto a greased baking sheet.

**WATER CHESTNUTS,** a Chinese delicacy, come from water-grown plants and resemble chestnuts. When very fresh, they are crunchy and have a coconut-like flavor. After canning, they lose some flavor but stay crisp. They are delicious sliced, in salads or casseroles. Store leftovers covered in the refrigerator.

# Crunchy Tuna Bake

2 cans (3 ounces each) French fried onions
1 can (16 ounces) cut green beans, drained
2 cans (6½ ounces each) tuna, drained and
   flaked
1 can (8 ounces) water chestnuts, drained
   and cut into thirds
1 can (10¾ ounces) condensed cream of
   chicken or mushroom soup
¼ cup milk
3 tablespoons mayonnaise or salad dressing
½ teaspoon curry powder

Heat oven to 350°. Reserve ¼ cup of the onions. Mix remaining onions, the beans, tuna and water chestnuts. Mix soup, milk, mayonnaise and curry powder; fold into tuna mixture. Pour into ungreased 2-quart casserole. Cover and bake 30 minutes. Sprinkle with reserved onions and bake uncovered 5 minutes.    6 SERVINGS.

---

### POT LUCK!

For best results, always use the size and shape baking dish that is specified in your recipe. If your baking dish is too large, the liquid will evaporate and baking time will be affected. If it is too small, your casserole may bubble over in the oven. If your recipe calls for a cover and you do not have one, aluminum foil is a good substitute.

# Tuna-Tomato Polenta

¾ cup cornmeal
¾ cup cold water
½ teaspoon salt
¼ teaspoon garlic salt
1½ cups boiling water
1 can (15 ounces) tomato sauce
2 cans (6½ ounces each) tuna, drained and
flaked
1 medium stalk celery, chopped (about ½
cup)
¼ teaspoon dried basil leaves
¾ cup grated Parmesan cheese
Sliced ripe olives

Mix cornmeal, cold water, salt and garlic salt thoroughly in 1-quart saucepan. Stir in boiling water. Cook over medium heat, stirring constantly, until mixture thickens and boils, about 2 minutes. Reduce heat; cover and simmer 10 minutes. Spread cornmeal in ungreased baking dish, 11¾x7½x1¾ inches. Refrigerate until firm, about 8 hours.

Heat oven to 350°. Mix tomato sauce, tuna, celery and basil. Spread ⅔ of the tuna mixture in ungreased baking dish, 12x8x1¾ or 13½x8¾x1¾ inches. Cut cornmeal into 10 parts; place on tuna mixture in dish. Top cornmeal with remaining tuna mixture; sprinkle with cheese. Bake uncovered 25 minutes. Garnish with olives.    10 SERVINGS.

Cook the cornmeal in 1-quart pan. Spread in dish; refrigerate 8 hours. Mix tomato sauce, tuna, celery, basil.

Spread ⅔ of the tuna mixture in dish. Place pieces of cornmeal on sauce. Top with remaining sauce and cheese.

# Party Baked Beans

½ pound fully cooked ham, cut into ½-inch
  pieces
1 can (28 ounces) baked beans in molasses
  sauce, drained
1 can (17 ounces) lima beans, drained
1 can (15½ ounces) butter beans, drained
1 can (15½ ounces) kidney beans, drained
  Barbecue Sauce (below)
1 can (20 ounces) sliced pineapple, drained
  Paprika

Heat oven to 350°. Mix ham and beans in ungreased 3-quart casserole. Pour Barbecue Sauce on ham and beans. Bake uncovered 1¼ hours. Stir before serving. If beans are too liquid, let stand 10 minutes. Garnish with pineapple slices; sprinkle slices with paprika.    8 SERVINGS.

## BARBECUE SAUCE
⅔ cup light corn syrup
⅓ cup catsup
¼ cup vinegar
1 medium onion, chopped (about ½ cup)
1 tablespoon prepared mustard
½ teaspoon garlic powder

Mix all ingredients.

# Baked Beans with Pork

    1 pound navy or pea beans (about 2½
        cups)
    1 tablespoon vegetable oil
    5 cups water
    ½ pound pork boneless Boston shoulder, cut
        into ½-inch pieces
    1 medium onion, sliced
    2 cups water
    ⅓ cup dark molasses
    1 small carrot, grated (about ⅓ cup)
    2 tablespoons brown sugar
2½ teaspoons salt
    1 teaspoon dry mustard
    ¼ teaspoon ground sage
    ⅛ teaspoon pepper
    ⅛ teaspoon liquid smoke

Heat beans, oil and 5 cups water to boiling in Dutch oven. Boil 2 minutes; remove from heat. Cover and let stand 1 hour.

Heat beans to boiling; reduce heat. Cover and simmer until beans are tender, about 50 minutes. Drain, reserving 1 cup liquid (if necessary, add enough water to measure 1 cup).

Heat oven to 300°. Layer beans, pork pieces and onion slices in ungreased 3-quart casserole. Mix reserved liquid and remaining ingredients; pour over beans. Cover and bake 2 hours. Uncover and bake, stirring occasionally, 1½ hours.    8 SERVINGS.

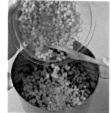

Simmer soaked beans until tender; drain. Layer the beans and corn. Mix flour, sugar, seasonings, tomato liquid; shake.

Stir the mixture into tomatoes; add green pepper. Pour on soybeans and corn; top with bread crumbs and cheese, then bake.

# Soybean Vegetable Casserole

6 ounces dried soybeans (about 1 cup)
4 cups water
1 teaspoon salt
1 can (16 ounces) whole kernel corn, drained
2 tablespoons flour
1 teaspoon sugar
¼ teaspoon Italian seasoning
⅛ teaspoon pepper
1 can (16 ounces) whole tomatoes, drained
    (reserve ½ cup liquid)
½ small green pepper, chopped (about
    ¼ cup)
1 cup soft bread crumbs
1 cup shredded Cheddar cheese (about
    4 ounces)

Heat soybeans and water to boiling in Dutch oven; boil 2 minutes. Remove from heat. Cover and let stand 1 hour.

Add salt to soybeans. Heat to boiling; reduce heat. Simmer uncovered until soybeans are tender, 2 to 3 hours; drain.

Heat oven to 375°. Layer soybeans and corn in ungreased 1½-quart casserole. Add flour, sugar, Italian seasoning and pepper to reserved tomato liquid. Shake in covered container; stir into tomatoes. Add green pepper. Pour on soybeans and corn. Top with bread crumbs and cheese. Bake uncovered 40 minutes.    6 SERVINGS.

# Spanish Noodle-Bean Bake

12 ounces uncooked noodles (about 4¼ cups)
1- pound ring bologna (casing removed)
1 large onion, chopped (about 1 cup)
2 medium stalks celery, chopped (about 1 cup)
1 small green pepper, cut into strips
1 tablespoon vegetable oil
1 can (8 ounces) tomato sauce
2 to 3 teaspoons chili powder
1 can (16 ounces) garbanzo beans*
½ cup sliced pitted ripe olives
1 can (16 ounces) whole kernel corn
1 can (11 ounces) condensed Cheddar cheese soup
Seasoned Cereal (right)

Prepare noodles as directed on package; drain. Heat oven to 350°. Cut bologna into ⅜-inch slices. Cook and stir bologna slices, onion, celery and green pepper in oil over medium heat until onion is tender. Stir in tomato sauce and chili powder.

Layer half each of the bologna mixture, noodles, beans (with liquid), olives and corn (with liquid) in greased 3-quart casserole; repeat. Spoon soup over top; sprinkle with Seasoned Cereal. Bake uncovered until hot and bubbly, about 40 minutes.    9 SERVINGS.

## SEASONED CEREAL
Crush 2 cups whole wheat flake cereal. Add 1 tablespoon grated Parmesan cheese and ¾ teaspoon garlic salt. Shake in plastic or paper bag to mix.

*1 can (16 ounces) kidney beans can be substituted for the garbanzo beans.

Crush cereal to make topping.

Pour into bag; add seasonings.

Close bag tightly; shake to mix.

Sprinkle crumbs on casserole.

Spread macaroni-frankfurter mixture in pie plate.

Top with tomato slices; pour on Parmesan cheese mixture.

# Hot Dog Macaroni

3½ ounces uncooked macaroni rings (about 1
    cup)
½ cup creamed cottage cheese (small curd)
1 egg, slightly beaten
¾ teaspoon salt
    Dash of pepper
½ cup shredded sharp Cheddar cheese
    (about 2 ounces)
2 frankfurters, cut into thin slices
2 medium tomatoes, sliced
1 egg
2 tablespoons grated Parmesan cheese
⅛ teaspoon dried oregano leaves

Cook macaroni as directed on package; drain. Heat oven
to 350°. Mix macaroni, cottage cheese, beaten egg, salt,
pepper, Cheddar cheese and frankfurter slices. Pour into
greased 9-inch pie plate. Arrange tomato slices on top. Mix
egg, Parmesan cheese and oregano; pour over tomatoes.
Bake uncovered until bubbly, 25 to 30 minutes.
5 SERVINGS.

---

### S-T-R-E-E-T-C-H IT WITH MILK!

Milk is the miracle food: a complete protein. You
can use it to s-t-r-e-e-t-c-h meat by including it in
sauces and soups, and it makes very little differ-
ence whether the milk you use is whole, skim, liquid or dry—provided that it is fortified with Vitamin D (and the skim or partly skim is fortified with
Vitamin A).

Evaporated milk is canned whole or skim milk
with a little more than half the water removed. It
provides twice as much protein as an equal
amount of fresh milk.

---

Add cheese to the uncooked macaroni in the casserole.

To crush potato chips easily, place in plastic bag and roll.

# Do-Ahead Macaroni and Cheese

7 ounces uncooked elbow macaroni
2 cups shredded Cheddar cheese (about 8 ounces)
1 can (11 ounces) condensed Cheddar cheese soup
1¾ cups milk
1 jar (2 ounces) sliced pimiento, drained
¾ teaspoon salt
1 cup crushed potato chips
Chicken-Pepper Sauce (right)

Mix all ingredients except potato chips and Chicken-Pepper Sauce in greased 2-quart casserole or baking dish, 8x8x2 inches. Cover and refrigerate up to 24 hours.

■1 hour 30 minutes before serving, heat oven to 350°. Stir macaroni mixture; sprinkle with crushed potato chips. Cover and bake 1 hour. Uncover and bake 20 minutes. Serve with Chicken-Pepper Sauce.    4 TO 6 SERVINGS.

## CHICKEN-PEPPER SAUCE

 1 package (about 1 ounce) chicken gravy
   mix
½ cup water
½ cup dairy sour cream
 2 tablespoons chopped green pepper
   Paprika

Heat gravy mix, water, sour cream and green pepper to boiling, stirring constantly. Sprinkle with paprika.

# Vegetable Lasagne

1 carton (24 ounces) creamed cottage cheese
2 eggs
3 tablespoons snipped parsley
¼ teaspoon salt
2 packages (10 ounces each) frozen chopped broccoli, thawed and drained
½ teaspoon salt
½ teaspoon garlic salt
8 ounces lasagne noodles, cooked and well drained
12 ounces sliced Monterey Jack cheese
1 cup grated Parmesan cheese
12 to 14 slices bacon, fried until limp

Heat oven to 350°. Mix cottage cheese, eggs, parsley and ¼ teaspoon salt. Sprinkle broccoli with ½ teaspoon salt and the garlic salt. Layer half each of the noodles, cottage cheese mixture, broccoli, cheese slices and Parmesan cheese in ungreased baking dish, 13½x8¾x1¾ inches; repeat. Arrange bacon slices on lasagne as pictured. Bake uncovered about 30 minutes.     8 TO 10 SERVINGS.